SPIRIT WELL

Joel White

SPIRIT WELL. Copyright © 2023 by Joel White. All right reserved. No part of this book may be used or reproduced in any manner whatsoever without written permission except in the case of brief quotations embodied in critical articles and reviews. For information, address Joel White at https://www.joeljwhite.com/contact.

ISBN 979-8-9898105-1-2 (Softcover)
ISBN 979-8-9898105-0-5 (eBook)

CONTENTS

PREFACE	VI
Good Water	1
Wings to Fly	2
Bitter Aftertaste	3
Pink Roses	4
Family is Thine	5
Why Shelter	6
Pursuing Refinement	7
Fight Well, or at Least Fight	9
Blade of Light	10
To the Grasslands	11
Dreams Come Again	12
Council of Clouds	13
Blessed Boldness	14
Play or Chains	15
Help Me Build	17

Stifling Spirit	18
Please Just Dance	19
Fire Starters	21
Promise Journey	22
Royal Warriors	23
Summer Years	24
Sing in Trials	25
Word Storms	26
Reverie of Decades	27
Discourse of Specters	28
Lament of Praise	29
Heart Ablaze	37
Inner Symphony	38
A Child Again	39
Remembering a Life	41
Park Bench Doxology	42
Generation Lovesick	43
Poet Dream	45

Wild Ones	46
Those That Flow With Joy	47
Death to Silence	48
The Dancing Warrior	49
Wholeness	50
Soul Speak	51
Lullabies	53
Closeness That Heals	54
Don't Spill the Tea	55
Sickening Self	56
Life of Prayer	57
After it Breaks	58
Tell the Stories	59
Submitted Things	60
Popcorn Plays	61
Thanks, Blessings, and More	62
ABOUT THE AUTHOR	64

PREFACE

I enjoy poetry and beautiful words, and language. I've dabbled in poetic scribblings before, to see if I could do it, and to express deep thoughts and emotions that could not be adequately processed in a typical journal entry. To write several poems, if you can call them that, in a collection to be published had never really crossed my mind. So why? And why now, especially as I am a filmmaker and not formally trained in the technical structure and formulations of meter, rhyme, and stanzas?

As I was praying during a difficult season of life, I felt a well of many things that I wanted to say, but could not yet articulate, swirling within me, waiting to be drawn to the surface. I wrote a poem or two, hoping it would be cathartic and help order some of my thoughts. Not only was it enjoyable and a relief, it was much more. I felt the peace of God in the process. And in the peace, it was as if I was fully alive in the midst of a calling. I had been having a strong desire to say certain things, in truth and in love, but I wasn't sure of how to say them. This poetry is born out of a revelation of deep calling unto deep, and I pray, for such a time as this.

My hope is to bring light, joy, beauty, and truth into your life. We do not have to succumb to the darkness of this world. Rather, we should fervently desire and look for the goodness of the Lord in the land of the living. So look here, and I hope that you will see. Look here, and I hope you will be encouraged. Read awhile, and be commissioned to partner in the cultivation of God's goodness.

Many thanks and blessings to you, dear reader!

Joel White

Good Water

Pittering rain, the humble companion of my
    solitude.
The intentional channeling of the water of my soul.
Tonight I find a place to observe its course.
Should this be so difficult?

It moves all the same, to a destined place.
I want to see it, perchance it's possible.
Do my currents lack sound, or am I deaf?
If hearing has escaped, remove my ears so I will be
    a target.

Let all streams flow with purpose and full
    character.
The tunes must play so the taste isn't lacking.

Wings to Fly

Is it time to fly?
I can never deny
My heart will try
Despite my cry
When I fall from the sky.

I don't ask why
When the chance is nigh
Instead of fly
My lows are high.

And when I sigh
The days go by
Whether I lie
Or let fear die.

It's time to fly.

Bitter Aftertaste

I know what will happen. Why is this difficult? It should be easy. At least, easier now. How does the taste kindle, attempting to become a fire? One that burns. I know the heat will not keep me warm. The maddening melting leaves me cold. Frigid loneliness intensifies with the aftertaste. No matter how many promises are made, the cheap sweetness is always bitter.

Pink Roses

Decades now, from when my heart delighted in the
    sight.
Roses in the bush by the small front porch.
Petals like her cheeks, bloomed in the light.
Thorns like steal, they pierced to scorch.

Their scent is present, but only in my mind.
Pressed against her face, her smile stays.
What joy this brings, these memories are kind.
Bless my hope, to tell children of these days.

Family is Thine

The woods of endless summer revel in their blessing. Housing those seeking refuge, the glory of the season becomes their raiment. How is such a thing possible? Many are only familiar with winter. Some have skipped with the passing summer. Now they carry the endless rays beyond these woods. Whether or not they ever return, the woods have established their place evermore. Upon the first greeting, they became kin.

Why Shelter

Why shelter, you're here for me. Warmer than the winds, but colder than the furnace. I'll make it through. Hours pass, days become opponents. Shelter, how do I stay? Nearly over, this contemptible plight; I will break ground to quicken my pace. What is wrong, shelter, why do I desire to escape you? Arduous nothingness courts me. Such an ignorant advance. I will face the desolate ice before betraying the creed. Why shelter, I may return or find another. I remain grateful, though I pray to find a place without you.

Pursuing Refinement

To be outside and run so freely,
Pushing myself to unknown lengths,
Is a comforting memory I hold so deeply,
Reminding me to seek newfound strengths.

Climbing trees, so naturally inclined
I move quickly to find the place
Where my reach ends and I am resigned
To pause for a moment and take in the space.

Pursuing skills to make a way,
The hours become days and quickly years.
I keep going, trying not to sway.
A new victory, the path now clears.

Faith wells, I move towards the unknown.
I must be ready, I've worked so hard.
Beauty yet to behold, from what was sown
Becomes gall in my mouth, it leaves me scarred.

I try my best, I know what's right.
This pressure mounts, do You even see me?
This is all for You, restore my sight,
The path has darkened and confounds me deeply.

My spirit fades, strength is gone.
Arrogance, fear, and dimming faith
Stir inside, it's hard to move on.
I lay here now, a desperate wraith.

I hear Your voice, it sparks a flame.
Mercy and peace find me low
On this floor of tears, never the same.
Hope is planted and begins to grow.

Take everything, if You must.
What remains is for You.
A life of sacrifice, rested in trust,
Is what I need, for You are true.

Fight Well, or at Least Fight

Fight for what you believe in.
Fight for those who are lost.
Fight for truth and purpose.
Fight like there's a cost.

Fight when they say, "Give up."
Fight like you don't fear death.
Fight because you've trained.
Fight for every breath.

Fight when hope seems distant.
Fight when you're weak at best.
Fight for those who hunger.
Fight for love and rest.

Blade of Light

My dangerous companion, how grateful I am for you. What a beautiful reminder is your edge that I am capable. You've grafted to my side, becoming an extension of my being. I remember the toil of your hammering. It was worth your initial form. You shone like silver stars. Your appearance, so pure, was like perfectly tempered glass.

You fought for me in the darkness; cutting away enemies and illuminating my path. I chose other companions for the journeys ahead. I mistakenly neglected you. I became cold and my light dimmed. Covered in rust, my edge was blunt.

Even so, you never abandoned me. You cut me well. The burn of your incisions quickly warmed me. I see your light as I did the first time, although better than before.

To the Grasslands

No wind against my cheek; a dead calm.
A bland color, it goes on for miles.
Hiding in a cave; the land of a psalm.
Remember the promise, face the trials.

A place of green; memory gives birth.
Days so distant; a tempest of time.
The quest for redemption, leads to this earth.
What desperate hope, I hear it chime.

Battles made way; the grass still grows.
Air of home, anchors my soul.
How blessed am I, my heart glows.
This land I know; I again feel whole.

Dreams Come Again

How oft I did dream as a child.
Every night, a play for my own viewing.
Odd characters, and stranger stories, rippled.
Grandeur and apocalyptic paintings, too real.
Eagerly desired gifts of waking.
Light of memory mingles with future.
Anticipatory writings, a declaration of my heart.
Fade, fade, fade the whispers of colors.
Blank years of hours strung through effort.
A chance notice points to lack in the land.
Which gates closed relationship?
My requests go up for company in the watches.
What's this? Images begin to trickle.
A forgettable dream, with unforgettable presence.
The beginning of hope brings cultivation.
I dream again, therefore I must honor the Giver.

Council of Clouds

Voluminous elders gather in the fire sky.
They seat themselves in the circle of unity.
"Important business!" They thunder sigh,
As the council begins their discourse in humility.

Each speaks his own language and is understood
    by all.
Vinya speaks in water and pleads compassion.
In turn, Ressa speaks shadow, illuminating a fall
That comes swiftly, hiding desperation.

Medis expresses concern in words of lightening,
Hoping his siblings will complete previous tasks.
Voices swirl as decisions begin ripening.
"Shall we close this council?" The eldest asks.

All agree and prepare their hearts,
For the part they will play in the time to come.
Etum gathers the words; the tumult starts.
He dances, preventing those below from becoming
    numb.

Hope is restored in the planes and heavens.
The desolate realm is now blessed and bountiful.
Communion above and below is the source which
    leavens
The elders spirits; they anticipate their next council.

Blessed Boldness

A place worth seeing beyond a vision
Exists for pilgrims far and near.
You must go, take up the mission
For the hour is nigh that this land becomes clear.

Two swords, double-edged, one to take.
Cowardice, one called, crusted in blood.
Boldness, the other, lit with flames its make.
Either choice will bring a flood.

To trust divine wisdom from God's own hand
Or conjure weightless pagan teachings,
You must decide how to travail for the land.
As did Christ, prepare to face many beatings.

A blessed choice, now it starts!
For boldness alights on others with His favor.
Should we ever doubt to steel our hearts,
Let that of the blessed Son be ours to savor.

Play or Chains

Fizzy pop orange, childhood elixir
Jumping up and down, so many stickers
I wanna go outside, play until the moon sleeps
Living like a ninja, kickin' heads for keeps

Can't hold me down, I fight like I play
Big breath, strong chest, every second of the day
Can't hold me down, these chains are lame
Don't want 'em, don't need 'em, they're breaking
   like clay

Skate shop wheels, flying like a bird
Punk song hero, wild as a herd
More to this than tricks, ankle flick strokes
Emerald eyes gleam, the fanning flame stokes

Can't hold me down, I fight like I play
Big breath, strong chest, every second of the day
Can't hold me down, these chains are lame
Don't want 'em, don't need 'em, they're breaking
   like clay

Croak like jester, roar like a lion
Battle in the matrix, keep my eyes on Zion
Chains cutting deep, none of this can stay
The King showed up, looked at me, "Let's play"

Can't hold me down, I fight like I pray
Big breath, strong chest, every second of the day
Can't hold me down, these chains all break
Don't want 'em, don't need 'em, watch me play all day

Help Me Build

This can't be it. Every day is the same. Every task is the same. I have a new idea. They don't want to hear it. I just want a chance. It's too different. I'll take it with me. So many hoarders. Where's the trust? I don't betray people. I let them see. Is there no reciprocation? I want to work with others. It's inevitable and impossible; a sobering paradox. My vision has value. Is your vision like mine? I see the value. Now is the time, as it always is; building relationship to build posterity. Please, help me build.

Stifling Spirit

Too many thoughts,
Never ending plots,
Are taking the spots.
Am I calling the shots?

Something's the matter.
There's so much clatter.
I hear the latter.
Will I be here after?

What do I do?
I've tried, it's true,
But I haven't a clue.
Where do I find You?

My spirit cries free.
Took awhile to see,
That You want to be
Ever present with me.

Please Just Dance

Amber hair flies across her face
In the night air where we just met.
Golden flecks in blue eyes chase
My heart in a place with no regret.

Biting her lip, a smile comes.
We share secrets, things become clear.
Words entangle, then she roams
Turning her face to hide a tear.

I try to comfort this glistening pearl,
Holding her close, her gaze meets mine.
Words of fire, my heart awhirl,
Listens carefully, searches for a sign.

How do I fight fearful woes
Of a gentle dove's unmerited burdens?
I plead her stop before it snows
And ask for hand as I lead to gardens.

Songs and green perish before her;
She stands and prays for peace to kindle.
I play a gambit in hopes to capture
Beauty's bane and end this riddle.

"Dance with me in the lavender air.
Let your heart be lead as love pursues.
Your steps a battle, with joyful flair,
Will partner with peace and kill these issues."

"I dance when happy," her soft reply
Makes me smile and press further.
"I think you're right, so now rely
On shining memories and teach this learner."

A fire burns, her skin now glows.
Moving softly, transforms herself
From helpless child with dainty rose
To warrior queen, a fairy elf.

Tears pass over blushing lips.
A ruby smile catches me up
In a dream too real, met by ships;
I sail these oceans and drink this cup.

Cast about on waves of joy
We sway to music unheard by ear.
This weapon of grace she will always employ
To blaze the darkness and obliterate fear.

Fire Starters

We are the peacemakers, we are the fire starters.
Isn't that an oxymoron? Not if your heart is softer,
Than those who demand peace, yet play with a
    flame,
That they don't understand, but burns just the
    same.
No, not the same, because you see, it's a different
    fire.
They start theirs with the ground, but our source is
    a little higher.
I do not wish to obfuscate or befuddle anyone's
    good meaning,
But I do hope to point out that truth married with
    conviction will not soon be leaving.

Promise Journey

"I will take care of you," echoes in my ears and lives in my heart.
I ask, "Is there more?" And plead "Where to start?"
I want to know the answers, but I'm hesitant to go and find.
I can't kid myself anymore that if I stay here they'll just pop into my mind.
Focused and resolute, I journey along this road, believing it will not consume me.
Tears streaming down my face, they assure me of living promises, and I know that I am free.

Royal Warriors

There was a time when we fought battles like Kings
    and Queens.
I'm afraid now we don't even know what it means,
To step forward in full raiment and awarded
    power,
Bleeding forgiveness and grace to those who would
    see us cower.
Reach to the One who would help you stand.
It's blessed to take hold, though you pierced His
    hand.
Be assured, sorrow and pain are to be had in a
    warrior's quest,
And though fighting may seem exhausting, the
    victories will bring rest.

Summer Years

What if I said I miss those days
Of summer bliss and moonlit plays?
When all was uncertain and yet so clear,
We'd break through walls, confounding fear,
Stealing looks to give them back,
Rivers of sweet tea drunk with the pack
In diner days of myths retold,
Roaring like lions to never grow old.
Will you find me when I've gone away
To a place where I said I'd be someday?
Maybe it's better you're in the past
Holding memories, built to last.
What if said I miss these days
Full of dreams, yet to be played?

Sing in Trials

When trials come and dragons sneer, will you sing with sacred temperament, undaunted? For the sake of the young, humble yourself like a child and let the joyful edges of your song clear a way for them. Do not worry about your fate, for you know the promise in the melody. Those who dare challenge your granted authority, challenge the One who gives it, bringing ruin upon their own heads.

Word Storms

All these words surround me, trying to find their place. Whispering, shouting, biting, and lying, what's their game? Making promises and denouncing others, sounding like truth. Now is the time, as it always will be, to speak fire to the waves.

Reverie of Decades

Years add up, hopscotch and orange pop.
Blood spills, paint the story with scars.
Games of adventure, a ten stop shop.
So real and so quick, lidless jars.
Dilettante youth, a soirée of clowns.
Breaking ribs, hoping to breathe.
No makeup, just happy frowns.
Collegiate arrogance; burned that wreath.
Shadows came, flying from light.
A dance with fear; taking the lead.
Digital celluloid, honest insight.
Fiery grace, third degree, please heed.
Still onstage, you know my creed.

Discourse of Specters

A brush of fancy.
"Do you enjoy it here?"
"Everything is different, but it's nice."
"Would you like to go somewhere new?"
….

An opening question.
"Do you enjoy your service?"
"Very much. Do you serve?"
"I do."
"Can we talk tomorrow?"
….

A bold decision.
"Would you like to meet with me?"
"…"
"I'll travel to your land."
"…"
"I'd like to know your nature."
……..

Lament of Praise

A lament of praise..
Reveries of days, decades, places, and people.
Where are the new memories?
I haven't forgotten how to dance.
I don't think..

"Hi, how are you?"
"So nice to meet you!"
"Would you like to run with me?.. Possibly share a meal with me?.. Maybe really talk with me?"

A conversation..
Such a beautiful thing.
Where did they go?
Intentional words standing on intrepid meaning.
Bleeding spirit and emotion, wrapped in bandages of levity.
I keep trying but..
"I gotta go."
Full stop.
"We'll touch base."
 Ring, ring?
Yeah right.

Go through the motions.
Sing a song of praise.
Momentary relief for a choir boy's pain.
Lord, I need your help.
It's difficult to hear You.
Why?..
Keep going.
You can do this.
A sinister thought, or a corrupted perception?

Put in the work.
Clock in.
Follow the rules.
Keep the peace.
Real peace?
Stay focused.
Hustle, hustle.
Next event.
Next class.
Next service.
Next glass.
A screen..
But what does this mean?

Something aches.
Should I lament?
I think I'll praise.
Moving right along.
So many people.
Too many people.
Too many people to feel this way.
What have I done wrong?
I played the niceties.
Offered more.
With a stinging smile, it falls through their fingers.
Hold on.
It's ok.
You can't force this.
There's too many people.
Too many to not find them.
To find the ones who run.

So, I'm lonely.
Here's a lament.
Especially for You.
Can You hear it?
Cause I'm still struggling.
Struggling to hear You.
Struggling to feel You.
If I cry really loud, will my heart be appealing to You?
Of course You care, I'm just perplexed, vexed, and apparently distressed.

I need a distraction.
No, something real.
A pretty girl?
Let's see what happens.
Intentional words, and what do you know?!
A real response!
Wait a minute..
No, three days.
Now two weeks.
I'd love to laugh just to feel bleak.
Stop, don't think like that.
Look, more pretty girls.
Pretty girls everywhere..
Who cares?
I guess I do.
But I wish I didn't.
That's not true..
Do I want it to be?
What does that even mean?
I'm sick of this vanity.
This overwhelming insanity.
Hanging over like a canopy.
Making me feel raggedy.
Playing in a never ending tragedy..
I know.. that's not reality.

Lights out..
Where am I?
A prayer?
Ok, I'll try..
I said I'll try.
I'm sorry, it's just that You know it all.
And I still can't feel You.
What do I need to do?
Will I be able to do it?
I've never felt this weak.
I can't even describe it.
Please let me know You're here.
Please.
Please!
I'm burning, but not with passion.

I'm in Your house now, with a lacerated chest.
Everyone can see.
Incapable of hiding it.
Not that I should.
Surgery starts and You break me in pieces.

What's left?..
Back to basics.
Starting from scratch.
Cut out the lies.
Don't worry about conversations.
Talk to Him.
Don't worry about the motions.
There's no need to impress.
There's no need to hustle.
It's time to rest.
Break the screen.
Clear your mind.
No more distractions.
Don't worry about relationships.
The light is on.
Time for truth.

Truth, truth, truth.
I see Your words.
I hear Your words.
Wait!..
This is it!
How did I not see it before?!
I was too busy.
It's You!
It's all about You!
Not what I can do.
Not where I go.
Not who I know.
I lay it all down.
I surrender.
I praise You!
And You alone.
My mind knows You, but my spirit missed You.
Hear my groaning!
I made idols.
I see that now.
Please forgive my arrogance.
To check the boxes.
To say the right things.
To be in the right places.
What does it matter, if I can't have You?
O Lover of my soul.
I'm burning again.
My heart's on fire.
Your Spirit sears me.
And it's welcome.
The flames bring healing..
Yes.. healing.
I remember You O Healer.

What kindness is this?
That I should obtain such a holy gift.

In lamentation, You gave me praise.
My spirit understands and my being is at peace.
I know now that I will see the goodness of the Lord
    in the land of the living.
A fervent desire.
Thank You for never leaving me.
I wasn't abandoned.
I was pursued.
I will pour myself out before You, so You can fill me
    up.
Thank You for hearing my lamentation, but
    moreover thank You for accepting my praise.

Heart Ablaze

Please accept the incense of my burning heart.
Bless the flames, stoke them as You will.
I want a pure desire, so I may play my part
To honor You with every gift, every skill.

Storms have come yet the embers still glow.
Warmth so faint, are they fading away?
Can this field be kindled; is it time to go?
Rivers from my eyes plead for Your play.

You give assurance, my heart always burned.
Your beauty untamable, catches it agaze.
My deepest longings in Your flames yearned
So I ask earnestly, set my heart ablaze!

Inner Symphony

The incredulity of my symphony
Has given me an epiphany.
Thinking words and saying thoughts that are rising
   up inside of me,
Though they are met with irony,
No less give me peace.

The effusive treasures of my spiritual hide-a-key.

A Child Again

Do you remember the warmth of the sun,
Waking you up and calling you?
The crisp, fresh air and the dewy grass?

The days that brimmed with adventure around
    every conceivable corner,
Wrapping you in blankets of wonder,
Played your games and revealed their own.

To what end did you suffer selfishness for
    transactions?
You still play games, but there's no spirit of play.
Nobody wins.
What wakes you now?

Pale light on foggy roads,
A match made in confusion.
Shallow minutes of endless hours pile up and keep
    falling.
I've been there,
Swimming in cantankerous obliviousness to the
    tears of my heart.

What had I become?
Where did my freedom go?
Longing for my first love lacerated my inner being.

Yet, though it felt like it,
I never forgot how to be childlike.
I never forgot how to dream.
So, even now, I run into His arms,
With groanings that become streams, and streams a
    song.
I become as a child,
Like we were told,
And find the peace of then, but greater now,
And lay down the shadows of my pride.

Remembering a Life

When all is said and done,
Will you notice that I've come and gone?

When memory and mirth meet,
Will you smile and get on your feet?

When I cried, when I tried, when I lied,
What kept you from running to hide?

When we sang and forever played,
Did it look like how you always prayed?

When all is said and done,
Will anyone weep when I am gone?

"But all IS said and done," you say,
"We have hope, freedom, He made a way."

"Tears will flow, with grief tender,
But so much more did He render!"

"He wept His blood for you,
You were born a goner, it's true."

"When all is said and done,
Will you rejoice in His glory and Kingdom come?"

Park Bench Doxology

Every night I go on a walk.
Every night I talk, talk, talk,
To myself and to You, it's never-ending.
I offer these words in hopes of mending.

I'm feeling better, but a wave has come.
I'm feeling discouraged, can I please go home?
This isn't what I planned, but I'll take the path.
Did I misstep again? Have I incurred Your wrath?

The floor is Yours, please speak freely.
The floor is Yours, I'm waiting desperately.
You spoke yesterday, I'm very grateful.
Nothing tonight? My heart is insatiable.

I make it to the bench and begin to ponder.
I make it and choose thoughts of wonder.
I struggle at first, but then they arrive.
The sweetest of memories now come alive.

Your goodness and mercy follows me!
Your goodness and mercy takes me outside of me!
I bare my soul, please fill my spirit.
I speak praises, I hope You can hear it.

Please forgive my grumbling, I know You are true.
Please forgive my stumbling. My Savior, it's You!
I needn't go forever and exhale an anthology,
I just pray You're glorified by this park bench
    doxology.

Generation Lovesick

Throw the blame up, throw the blame down.
Everywhere you look, a cherished frown.
It's not confusing, there's just no sense.
Seemingly bemusing, without recompense.

This generation is lovesick.

Be who you are, except for that.
It's really quite simple, you little rat.
Everything is good, but not your morals.
Trust in vanity and accept your laurels.

This generation is lovesick.

Your pain is unique, like none before.
There's no remedy so wage your war.
Blatant lies have become your dinner.
Ignore reality, O precious sinner.

THIS GENERATION IS LOVESICK!

You groan inside, yet choose to hide.
Light has come, lay down your pride.
Eternity in your heart, from the greatest of fathers.
His blood for yours, all sons and daughters.

Open your eyes, Generation Lovesick!

Blind no more, you still must choose
To wallow in the mire, or be let loose.
Your sickness will stay, no matter the choice,
But only one option will make you rejoice.

God bless Generation Lovesick!

Poet Dream

I had a dream once, that I met a poet.
I showed interest, but I think I blew it.
She was confused and questioned my intention.
"I write too," failed to make connection.

"Why are you a poet?" Caught me off guard.
Why bandy words with this curious bard?
"I have things to say," my quick reply.
She urged my words, "Please don't be shy."

I became nervous, yet wished to speak.
Her mysterious pleadings made me weak.
I soon woke up, very much perplexed.
What does it mean? Is the answer next?

Wild Ones

We are the Wild Ones,
We are the Fire Ones,
The dance until our feet break, praising through the tired, Ones.

We are the Honest Ones,
We are the Joyful Ones,
The persecuted servant family seeking for the orphans, Ones.

We are the Hopeful Ones,
We are the Loving Ones,
The bear your cross and follow Him, calling on His name, Ones.

The safe ones,
The chained ones,
The self-empowered fake ones?

That's not our cup, you see?
Now come and join the Wild Ones!

Those That Flow With Joy

Tears of pain flowed easily as a child.
I just wanted to be free and wild.

Tears of growth came during change.
They watered my foundation through the strange.

Tears of grief felt never-ending.
Unspeakable peace somehow residing.

Tears of suffering blurred my sight.
He saved me in the ocean and brought the Light.

Tears of joy are different today.
I used to laugh and glimmer rays.

Tears of joy find me still.
Content and thankful, I take my fill.

Tears of joy come forth from memory,
Swaddling my heart in crystalline tapestry.

Tears of joy surprise me here.
Woo me tender and bring your cheer!

Tears of joy float visions of tomorrow.
I see the goodness and lack of sorrow.

Tears have been confusing and wretched and splendid.
But perhaps they are a unique gift when with joy they are blended.

Death to Silence

I don't know how it happened…
The silence.
"You're so nice!" Stabs me quick.
I bleed a smile and manage my peace.
This kind comment covers me thick
In tameness unwanted, I'm ill at ease.

I made attempts…
To break the silence.
"That's not true!" Catches some attention.
A bewildered face quickly turns red.
Brimstone words explode with tension.
I become soft and filled with dread.

I listened to nonsense…
My heart yelled, "Silence!"
"Appease the childish," makes my blood boil.
I ignore the witchcraft as if not said.
I look to my allegiance but don't feel loyal.
If I'd stood my ground I could've at least bled.

It was the compromises…
A breeding ground for silence.
I will not live silent, now or ever!
I have too much to lose, to gain, to share!
Death to the quiet, soul-crushing lever!
I will speak truth loudly with intrepid flair!

The Dancing Warrior

He hears the lark and knows it's time.
Savoring the chirps, he girds his waist.
Prepared for battle, the man must climb
To the sacred place with vivacious haste.

A warrior, yes, though gentler than most,
At the ancient courtyard prepares his art.
Feet now bare, he mans his post
Skimming the stones, flames in his heart.

The Spirit moves him, starting the flow.
The earnest steps of graceful warfare
Birth resolve with starry glow.
A dance of fervor, fantastically fair.

Raging this tempest clears a way.
The warrior's gift now joins the trail
Of valiant servants, that did dragons slay.
His offering of beauty will always prevail.

Wholeness

The Holy God filled a hole in my heart.
Now I am whole and not just in part.
Wholeness in body, soul, and spirit
Calls me to holiness; I can hear it.

Soul Speak

"People don't talk that way anymore."
How did you say it?..
Out of boredom?
Out of disgust?
I like words.
Better yet, I like their arrangement.
A melancholy phrase with a sparrow's melody.
The enchanting juxtaposition, such a a delight!
Were you really unmoved?
Your ears heard, but did your heart listen?

"People don't talk that way anymore!"
Was it anger?..
Confusion?
Maybe there was a misuse of beauty.
Was it weaponized against you?
Don't play the villainous victim.
Your vigor suits you in the truth that seared you.
Devour the bread.
Forgive the one who threw it.

"People... don't talk that way anymore."
Sadness, perhaps?..
Or longing?
Be of good cheer!
Fastidious fellows are incumbent to remunerate.
So please, join this remnant of play.
It's serious business, you know?
Serious as in the nature of kisses and hugs.
The paradox of preposterously perplexing
    paradigms of joy.

"People don't talk that way anymore," you say.
My dear friend..
It's high time, as ever before, with great candor and delight that we should.

Lullabies

Sing me a lullaby before you go.
Just one more, so my dreams will glow
With beauty bright and brimming hope.
I'll carry it with me like a sacred rope.

Should nightmares come and lease their terrors,
I shall lasso them and exploit their errors.
They dissolve in the dewy lullaby's ringing.
The joy of resting in endless singing.

I sing today, like you did for me.
They ask for two more, so we settle for three.
Giggles and snores now breeze on by
Filling the night with the sweetest lullaby.

Closeness That Heals

Keep me close.
Let me feel Your nearness.
I'm tired.. o so tired.
I know I'm not alone when I'm by myself.
Loneliness tempts my flesh though.
… Why?
You've taught me how to keep going.
And when my heart is heavy and my feet are stone,
    You lift me up.
You are my strength.
I hold fast to this revelation of Your love.
Forgive my wavering.
Have mercy on my actions.
I used to put on a show, as if everything was
    alright.
Sanctimonious chicanery border-lining on
    blasphemy.
Keep me far from past failings, I pray.
Please.. Keep me close.

Don't Spill the Tea

A delicious brew for me and for you
Warms the cockles and begins conversation.
Aroma and flavor of words so new
Keep us from poking tepid consternation.

Another cup! To the brim with green.
Steady now, savor every drop.
Delightfully sip and peacefully glean
Joyous moments where darkness stops.

There's no time to waste on gossip or slander.
We intend to glorify God, you see?
With choice words to illuminate His grandeur,
All the while not spilling the tea.

Sickening Self

Narcisism!
Glorification of self-deprecation.
Let's take a selfie, but stand behind me!
Everyone must see that I'm hurting, but pretending otherwise.
I'm so special.
Everyone does the same, but not like me.
I use heavy contrast.
I'm famous, I'm famous!
So many views and all the hearts.
What am I famous for?
For being myself!
What do you mean like everyone else?
I'm special!
Wait, no not them!
Look at me!!
Are you looking at yourself?
Where is everyone?
We're all here, but no one is in attendance.
A collective simulation.
If I'm famous in the matrix, am I loved here?
.. Am I loved?
I am?
I must know this Love!
Help me break these alters of algorithmic platforms of peril.
To make You famous delights my soul.
I nearly missed it, others must know.
When self dies, I am found in Christ.
His resurrection brings new life.

Life of Prayer

Teach me how to pray,
To pray without ceasing,
In a manner that is pleasing.
I will lift my voice despite my stubborn reasoning.

I need to pray,
That's for certain.
As I speak You unload my heavy burdens.
Lead me back to Your Garden,
Where I'm watered by the Blood and find Your pardon.

With faith I must pray,
No need to take chances.
Help my unbelief in my circumstances.
Drown me with hope as the enemy advances.
Bless me with trust as I praise with dances.

Without words I pray,
My spirit cries for me.
You understand the incoherence of my plea.
Holding my marrow, you intercede so I'll be free.
How amazing, that You pray for me!

Help me listen as I pray,
Your Word gives life, more than anything I could ever say.

After it Breaks

My heart breaks, but I'm not special.
It's part of life, all must partake
In the pains that come with which we wrestle.
They drive through us like a wooden stake.

So what do we do when the shattering comes?
Mine has broken many a time.
So many pieces, a great many sums
Scattered about like a familiar rhyme.

It's not a secret, I'll tell you now
How every repair will always fail.
Until you recognize that you must bow,
Mending awaits with the King, so HAIL!

Tell the Stories

Time to tell a story, act it out!
Around the campfire, watch and listen.
Heroes and villains battle and shout
As children squeal and eyes glisten.

Time to tell a story, pick up a brush!
Strokes of color reveal a place
Where all are welcome in the rush
Of exuberant play that gives us chase.

Time to tell a story, write it down!
Plan the plots, fill in the blanks.
An enthralling tale, a shining crown,
Rests on many, filled with thanks.

Time to tell a story, record the scene!
Filters and lights, actors and pages
Bring the life intended for screen.
Many great films decimate cages.

Time to tell a story, however you choose!
Step out in faith, release your narrative.
Quality is needed, there's no time to lose.
Start the chapter, it's time to give.

Submitted Things

There are so many things I want to do.
I want to write beautiful stories,
To act them out especially for you,
To make you happy and forget your worries.

I want to travel and see many wonders.
Bring me to places where work is needed.
Give me grace despite my blunders.
Let me sow and reap what was seeded.

I hope to build a haven for the weary,
To give them a bed and a place to eat.
Conversations and song to heal the dreary,
Will produce oil for the washing of feet.

What I want most of all is found in my King.
A submitted life, dipped in His glory,
Compels me to praise, dance, and sing.
I want to live for the Author of my story.

Popcorn Plays

I put on the vest for the popcorn plays,
Sweeping and cleaning for days upon days.
Laughs with friends behind silver screens
Kept us united through dramatic scenes.

Gossip and heartbreak were featured players.
I cut their lines with many prayers.
A unique time to grow in a great many ways.
I look fondly on my days in the popcorn plays.

Thanks, Blessings, and More

Thank you for your time and making it this far.
I hope you enjoyed what I placed in this jar.
These words are for you and for many others.
I hope by now we have become brothers.

Sisters please, be encouraged by this verse.
Take hold of the truth and break a curse.
Your voice is needed, especially today.
Take up the reins, release what you would say.

I pray what was written leaves you blessed.
I hope you are lifted and no longer stressed.
My heart has run over onto these pages.
May God be glorified as this sea rages.

ABOUT THE AUTHOR

Joel White is an actor/filmmaker from Fort Worth, Texas. He started telling stories from a young age and enjoys the positive impact they can have on people's lives. After getting a bachelor's degree in Radio, Television, and Film from the University of North Texas, Joel has passionately continued his career in the arts. His conviction that art is meant to draw people to the beauty of God and to glorify Him is ever increasing. Joel earnestly desires to create art that blesses people and ultimately extols the Lord.

YouTube: www.youtube.com/@joeljwhite
Instagram: www.instagram.com/joeljwhite
Twitter: www.twitter.com/joeljwhite
Facebook: www.facebook.com/joelwhiteofficial
www.joeljwhite.com

www.ingramcontent.com/pod-product-compliance
Lightning Source LLC
LaVergne TN
LVHW041309080426
835510LV00009B/920